It's Time to Talk About It.

Trauma Hidden in Plain Sight

It's Time to Talk About It.

Trauma Hidden in Plain Sight

By: Shaquita Moore

"It's Time to Talk About It: Trauma Hidden in Plain Sight" Copyright © 2023 (Shaquita Moore)

ISBN: 979-8-9869787-4-1

EBOOK ISBN: 979-8-9869787-7-2

All rights reserved. No part of this book may be reproduced, stored in a retrieval system, or transmitted in any form or by any means, electronic, mechanical, recording, or otherwise without written permission from the author.

Scripture quotations marked "KJV" are taken from the Holy Bible, King James Version (Public Domain). Scripture quotations marked "AMP" are taken from the Amplified® Bible, Copyright © 1954, 1958, 1962, 1964, 1965, 1987 by The Lockman Foundation. Used with permission. Scripture quotations marked (NLT) are taken from the Holy Bible, New Living Translation, copyright © 1996, 2004, 2007 by Tyndale House Foundation. Used by permission of Tyndale House Publishers, Inc., Carol Stream, Illinois 60188. All rights reserved.

Published by: New Voice Books LLC

Website: nvpublishingco.com

Table of Contents

Dedication

Disclaimer

Forward

Chapter One: Jael's Short Story

Chapter Two: Trauma Defined

Chapter Three: Hidden Trauma Effects

Chapter Four: Nothing New Under the Sun

Chapter Five: Be Proactive

Chapter Six: Seek Help

Chapter Seven: Power of Words

DEDICATION

I'm dedicating this book to anyone who has been abused or experienced any form of trauma that may have altered their behavior and thinking pattern. I understand what it's like to be challenged with side effects of trauma and I want to share with every reader the principles on how to not only identify hidden trauma but also how to overcome it.

DISCLAIMER

This author is not a licensed Therapist; therefore, this book is not to be used to replace the care of legal mental health professionals. It is essentially a guide to assist you with identifying trauma. The author, however, discusses the importance of seeking help and provides a list of nationwide resources at the end of the book.

Forward

I had the pleasure of meeting Shaquita Moore during the Pandemic. I was drawn to her sweet spirit and love for God and his people. Shaquita has inspired me so much over the past couple of years. I have watched her grow in the things of God, as a mother, working full time, getting her degree, and authoring this book. Her desire to help women is evident in her book. Not only is she transparent but has a gift to help young women find out who they are in God and to heal from trauma.

I look forward to seeing her in discussions on her book with groups of women and see their lives transformed. Talking and sharing with her has helped me heal from trauma that I have been dealing with for years and gave me the courage to discuss it with a professional in my area. I am so appreciative of the gift Shaquita has given me to look deep within and confront the trauma I have experienced over the years. I pray others will have the opportunity to do the same for themselves and or their children so that future generations will be healed and set free from the bondage that has kept them stuck for years.

Gwen Johnson

In today's society the subject of trauma and abuse is taboo. Many children are suffering in silence. This often leads to behavioral challenges, inattentiveness, anger, insecurity, and aggression, just to name a few. They are often prevented from using their voices to tell a trusted adult due to shame, guilt, or simply being told not to tell anyone. In "It's Time to Talk About It", Shaquita walks us through the process of speaking out and walking in freedom.

Shaquita is an exceptional Social Worker, mother, sister, and daughter. I have the honor of her being one of my best friends and Social Work Colleague. We grew up in the same town, Orrville, Alabama. As we become older, our relationship grew together in our faith and careers. Shaquita is a Master Level Clinician with such amazing knowledge, wisdom, and insight into mental health and trauma. She uses her platform to encourage, equip, and help others excel overcome adverse factors in their lives, including me. Shaquita is the epitome of breaking barriers and overcoming life challenges and trauma. She's an advocate for mental health support and how it aids in the healing process. Shaquita used these principles in her book to heal and grow and now she is sharing the wealth with others. Shaquita is disciplined, dedicated, and determined for generations to be free, healed, and whole. I encourage you to get a book for your sister, mother, brother, friend, church group, and school to talk about and identify the factors of trauma and abuse as well as utilize the resources in this book to receive mental health support and/or therapy.

Shaletha Robinson, LCSW

Chapter One

JAEL'S BRIEF SYNOPSIS

" And we know that all things work together for good to them that love God, to them who are the called according to His purpose."

Romans 8:28 KJV

WHO IS JAEL?

Jael is a 14-year-old female. Straight out of the womb she was at risk of adverse childhood experiences, her environment was polluted with drugs, perversion, gangs, and violence. She lost her mother at the age of five due to substance abuse. From the ages 6-7, Jael was molested by a friend of the family. This incident occurred when her father moved back to his mother's house temporarily.

With only one income in the household, Jael father could not afford to maintain the living expenses. Jael's grandmother who everyone called Big Momma, was a woman full of compassion, and love for her community. She was also known for her cooking. For three months Big Momma allowed a friend of her youngest son to live with them until he got back on his feet. Unknowingly to the family, Jael was just another bait to the young man.

During his last two months, residing at her grandmother house he would touch Jael in inappropriate places and tell her if she told someone no one would listen to her. Jael never could find the courage to say anything, and no one in the house discerned what was going on. For years Jael masked the pain that she was feeling from losing her mother and from being sexually abused.

Ponder on this question for a few seconds, are you allowing yourself to feel your feelings, and process your pain or are you wearing a mask to hide your pain as though it does not exist? In a later chapter you will discover what happens when trauma is left unaddressed.

After living with her grandmother for a few years, Jael's father finally decided to get married. Jael's father met Sonya, his new wife, at a country club. She has two daughters Zana and Dana. Zana was jealous of Jael. She thinks that Jael's father ruined their family, however, she is not aware that her own father committed adultery. Six years later after the wedding, everything was going well; until Jael was slapped in the face with another tragic event.

One day after school following Jael's 13th birthday, the school bus arrived at Jael's home. She looked out the window and saw people from the community standing by her fence. Once she got off the bus, when her feet hit the pavement, her heart dropped, as she saw her father lying on the ground in a puddle of blood. She had no words, only feeling emotionally numb. Her father was wrongfully shot by an unfamiliar suspect. As a result of her Father's death, she was left without a healthy support system. Jael's grandmother's health declined two years after they moved out, so she was left in the hands of her wounded stepmother.

FAST FORWARD A YEAR LATER ....

After a long summer break, Jael wakes up with excitement knowing in two days she will be starting her first day as a freshman at Kingdom High School. Most students dread going back to school, but for Jael school was her way of escaping from her dysfunctional family. After the death of her father, nothing was the same, her stepmother is not the nicest person anymore and Jael still does not have a good relationship with her stepsister Zana. Dana spends the majority of her time with her boyfriend, so Jael doesn't see her that often. Jael stated, "You would think that we would have gotten even closer after the death of my father but instead everyone is doing their own thing."

No one is excited that Jael is preparing for her first day of high school. Her best friend's mother took her shopping for school supplies and clothes. One morning Jael was in deep thought thinking about her first day of school. She wondered; will she be able to talk to her friends. What will she wear on her first day? What would her teachers be like and how is she going to decorate her first locker?

Out of nowhere, Zana interrupted Jael thoughts, she yelled, "Jael!!!! My mother said to get up and clean the kitchen and bathroom." Mind you It's 6 a.m. on a Saturday. Who wakes up that early to clean, not me, Jael thought to herself.

Jael stated, "I will be glad when school starts so I can get a break from this house." "What did you say?" asked Zana. Jael repeats herself. Zana who is 6 years older than Jael sarcastically asked, "Why are you so excited about school, it's not like you are smart anyway."

Instead of responding, she remained calm. Jael knew Zana couldn't handle her. One day she raised her voice to Zana and discovered that she was all bark and no bite. Jael stayed in bed for about 30 more minutes thinking to herself "Man there has to be so much more to life than this." Negative thoughts begin to overtake her mind "I'm tired of feeling inadequate, being overlooked, and neglected. I wish my father was here, I would have been better off in the system with someone that genuinely cared about me."

Though Jael is a resilient girl deep down inside she was broken, confused, and deprived of a normal environment. She started her morning off by remixing her favorite song by Amanda Perez using her thoughts to sing aloud. "God send me an Angel to wash the tears from my eyes. Send me an angel to heal my broken heart. All I do is hide from the pain deep inside. oh God, I need you to send me an Angel."

FIRST DAY AS A FRESHMAN

It's Monday! Her first day as a freshman at KHS. Jael was ecstatic to see her friends. "Tamar, Samara, Leah!" Jael screamed. She was so happy to reunite with all her friends. The girls joined together in a group hug. They have been best friends since the 1st grade.

Over the years they shared secrets that no one else knew. They all encountered some form of abuse and were unknowingly connected through their experience with trauma. Last year they were considered the fast girls in the eyes of the faculty and staff. Little did the staff know that they were broken and in need of divine guidance.

After taking hundreds of pictures the girls shared their schedules, somehow, they all are in different classrooms this year. They will only have two breaks together, snack and lunch. "Ring Ring Ring", the sound of the homeroom bell goes off, they all departed saddened at the drastic change of being separated.

Jael unhurriedly walked into her homeroom class. She scanned the room and noticed a vacant seat in the back row. After the tardy bell, her teacher Mrs. Clark walked into the classroom, closed the door, and welcomed the students. This was Mrs. Clark's first year of teaching, so she was super excited to get to know her first class.

As a warm-up assignment, Mrs. Clark asked the students to write down one thing they like about themselves, one thing no one knew about them, and what they want to be when they grow up. After the students wrote down their answers, she instructed them to all share what they wrote. The closer Mrs. Clark got to Jael's row the more anxious she became. Her palms started to sweat, and her stomach began to bubble. When it was her turn, she stood up and her legs began to shake uncontrollably.

At that moment Jael wanted to become a track star. Speaking in front of others isn't something she ever liked to do or felt she was good at. In this case, Jael couldn't run so she attempted to face her fears. Jael introduced herself and only shared what she wanted to be and immediately sat back down and sunk into her chair. Deep inside she was embarrassed and ashamed. Her classmates made fun of her without being aware of her internal battles. This is what often happens when individuals are not trauma informed. Mrs. Clark redirected her class and moved on to the next student.

Many are suffering in silence because of a lack of knowledge about mental health and the effects of childhood trauma. To an average person, Jael may be labeled as everything except for who she truly is. Some may think she's incompetent, or shy. However, on the inside, she is bold, resilient, smart, and unique.

After being molested and losing her mother and father at an early age, Jael developed moderate anxiety. Which became an anchor that hindered Jael from living a free social life.

4th Block

After what seemed to be the longest first day of school without the company of her friends. Jael finally made it to her last class which is Sociology. She scanned the classroom and noticed another vacant seat in the back row. As usual, she secured the back row seat.

Unexpectedly, Jael's teacher announced that everyone has assigned seats in alphabetical order. Jael immediately thought to herself, "Are we in the third grade?" She was displeased because her last name started with an A, so this meant she would have to sit in the first row. When Mrs. Deborah called Jael's name, she rolled her eyes and slung her backpack across her back. Instead of getting offended Mrs. Deborah waited to speak to Jael after class.

When the bell rang for dismissal Jael waited for everyone to leave out the classroom, before Jael stepped her feet out the door, Mrs. Deborah stopped her and said, "Jael I noticed that you were not too ecstatic about moving to the front." "Is everything ok?" Mrs. Deborah asked Jael. Jael responded, "No, I don't like sitting in the front because it makes me feel uncomfortable."

Mrs. Deborah knew that Jael was exemplifying an avoidance behavior. After realizing that Jael was battling with an internal issue Mrs. Deborah began to boost Jael's confidence by empowering her. She said to her, "You are a smart young lady with greatness on the inside of you." Jael rudely responded, "You don't know me."

Mrs. Deborah said, "I don't know you personally, but I see that you are an intelligent young lady, and you have a bright future ahead of you." Jael looked at Mrs. Deborah and said, "No one ever told me I was smart." Jael continues by sharing partial of her story with Mrs. Deborah, "It seems like I can't catch a break everyone I love has been taken away from me, my mother overdosed on opioids when I was 5, my father was murdered last year, nothing has been the same at home since my father died, and now I am separated from my friends."

Mrs. Deborah said to Jael "What you have experienced does not dictate who you are, there is so much more to life than what you see in your environment. What happened to your family is not your fault. Because you are standing here today means that you have a purpose, and you will be exposed to amazing things, that your mind won't be able to fathom. You will not be intimidated by the face or opinions of others; and you will learn to be your authentic self unapologetically." Tears immediately began to roll down Jael's cheek. For the first time, she finally felt like she belonged. For years Jael questioned her existence on earth.

After that conversation, Jael developed a relationship with Mrs. Deborah. She was more than just a teacher to her; she became a mentor and a mother figure that Jael dreamed of having. Just like that, God shifted Jael's destiny. Mrs. Deborah treated Jael as if she was her own, she made sure all her psychological needs were met and she also referred her to the on-campus Therapist. Jael's stepmother agreed to the service.

Leadership Matters

Educators play a major role in the development of our youth. Mrs. Deborah took the initiative to put her title to the side and she met Jael where she was. She saw that Jael was in a dark pit, and she knew that if she didn't pull her out it was a possibility that no one else would. So instead of allowing Jael to spend years in bondage repeating negative behavior patterns and limiting herself. Mrs. Deborah showed compassion to Jael because she knew what it felt like to be oppressed, rejected, and abandoned.

Mrs. Deborah grew up without a father figure in the home and she was molested around the same age as Jael. Mrs. Deborah didn't dare to tell her mother that she was molested until a day before she went off to college. For years she kept that inside and never received counseling until she was thirty. Mrs. Deborah knows from experience what it is like to grow up silently battling with trauma. Now she can be the person to Jael that she needed in high school. This is her way of being proactive with her at-risk scholars. Mrs. Deborah makes sure all her students not only receive what they need academically but also makes sure that her students are mentally and emotionally stable.

Many of you reading this book may not have the same background as Mrs. Deborah and Jael, but we all have experienced some form of direct or indirect trauma that has affected the way we think, live, and interact with others. It's important that we say something when we identify negative behavior patterns within those we are surrounded by daily. Your one act of showing compassion even if you don't understand can change the trajectory of someone else's life.

Healing Process

Three months into therapy Jael's outlook on life began to change, due to Jael's transformation her stepmother and sisters started counseling as well too. As a result, therapy shined a light upon hidden wounds within her household. Jael's stepmother never healed from being cheated on by her previous husband, so her wounds enlarged after the death of Jael's father. Therapy also exposed why Zana was so bitter. Zana, who is 17, shared with Jael that she envied her relationship with her father because her father neglected them even when they lived in the same home. She asked for forgiveness, but Jael had already forgiven her.

Zana also had unforgiveness in her heart towards her mother due to thinking that her mother was the reason her father abandoned them. When Dana, who is 19, started therapy, it was discovered that she was not in love; she was blind. Her boyfriend abused her and cheated on her multiple times, no one ever knew about the abuse because she masked her scars with Maybelline. After everyone addressed their hidden wounds the atmosphere of their home shifted. Now the family is spending more time together, healing, learning, and growing.

I truly believe that hidden traumas are the number one reason families are divided today, just think about your family lineage. What are some events that took place in your home or community, and everyone just turned a deaf ear to it? As I was typing this I was reminded of the saying; see no evil, hear no evil, speak no evil. This has to be the most foolish statement I ever heard one make, but this is what has happened or may be happening in many families today.

Dysfunction doesn't just occur over night. Because many choose to ignore evil, evil becomes more and more prevalent. Jael's life is proof that addressing hidden wounds is not just about receiving freedom for yourself. She tried all that she could to avoid informing her stepmother that she was seeking professional help for her mental health, but by law, Jael had to receive permission from a legal guardian first before starting services. Jael was shocked that her stepmother and stepsisters decided to receive counseling. Before moving to the next chapter, ask yourself this question. **Am I holding up someone else's healing process?** In a later chapter we will discuss the stigma around seeking help for our mental health but first, let's identify trauma.

Chapter Two

Trauma Defined

"He restoreth my soul: he leadeth me in the paths of righteousness for his name's sake."

Psalm 23:3 KJV

What is Trauma?

Trauma is described as an event or act that takes place and affects the psychological well-being of an individual.[1] Trauma is caused by the

---

[1] Center for Substance Abuse Treatment (US). Trauma-Informed Care in Behavioral Health Services. Rockville (MD): Substance Abuse and Mental Health Services Administration (US); 2014. (Treatment Improvement

loss of a loved one, natural disasters, accidents, traumatic brain injury, divorce, injustice, poverty, domestic violence, and abuse (sexual, physical, mental, emotional, and verbal). Depending on how frequently these events take place, the duration of the event trauma can be divided into three types: acute, chronic, and complex trauma.

Not everyone who experiences trauma suffers from long term side effects. You can view trauma-like taking medication, there are some medications that an individual can take that will cause temporary side effects such as diarrhea, headaches, and even drowsiness, but there are other medications that have long-term adverse effects that could put one at risk to having liver, brain, and kidney injury.

Protocol (TIP) Series, No. 57.) Section 1, A Review of the Literature. Available from:
https://www.ncbi.nlm.nih.gov/books/NBK207192/

Three Types of Traumas (Acute, Chronic, and Complex)

Before collating these terms with trauma let's first look at their original definition.

Acute: means to present or experience to a severe or intense degree.

Chronic: means an illness persisting for a long time or constantly recurring.

Complex: means consisting of many different and connected parts. [2]

Acute Trauma

Acute trauma refers to a one-time event that has a negative impact on an individual. This can be due to physical assault, sexual abuse, a car accident, or a natural disaster. Acute trauma

---

[2] Oxford Languages and google English Dictionary. (2023)

usually requires short-term treatment and therapy.

Chronic Trauma

Chronic trauma occurs from exposure to multiple types of physical trauma. Some potential causes of chronic trauma include sexual abuse, domestic violence, and physical bullying. With chronic trauma, the victims often have trust issues. Without trust, they lack the ability to form stable relationships. Chronic trauma often requires a longer duration of treatment.

Complex Trauma

Complex trauma is the result of exposure to multiple forms of abuse at a young age. Just to name a few, complex trauma can be caused by childhood abuse, emotional neglect, and domestic violence. Complex trauma impacts health, relationships, and individual job performance. It generally requires long-term treatment and therapy. [3]

From reading the three types of traumas, what type of trauma do you think Jael survived? If your response was complex, you are correct. Jael experienced multiple events of trauma which altered her cognitive thinking, behavior, and her personality. When signs of trauma are not identified or ignored it can eventually take a toll on a person's health, emotions, and life. There are many teens, young adults, adults, and seniors challenged with an illness that could have been prevented by revisiting their past and getting to the root of the events that altered their health.

For some, this is not the easiest thing to do but it causes more damage when trauma is suppressed rather than addressed. It's vitally important that every root linked to trauma in our

---

[3] "What are the 3 types of trauma?":
https://mhcsandiego.com/types-of-trauma/

life is exposed, uprooted, and destroyed Roots are so powerful, if any of you know anything about a plant when a plant dies often time the roots are still alive and can be used to produce more than what was visible. What am I trying to say is? It's a reason why you are always retreating in the middle of a confrontation, it's a reason why you are constantly having migraines, it's a reason why you always run when obstacles come, it's a reason you dim your light instead of shinning bright when a noble person enters your presence. You are right there is a reason, and that reason can be linked to trauma. It's time to get to the root of the issue and stop running.

When we don't get to the root of those things that are hidden, we will continue to grow but instead of springing up something beautiful the root of trauma springs up **depression, anxiety, high blood pressure, heart disease, migraines, stress, fear, relationship problems, sibling rivalry, jealousy, hate,**

bitterness, shame, negative mindsets, limitations, procrastination, low-self-esteem, communication problems, self-pity, and so much more.

Some individuals think that running solves everything. For example, many think that changing their environment or finding someone to fill the void would resolve the issue, however, it doesn't matter how far you go or what method you use to suppress the pain, it will never go away until you address the issue. If you don't deal with the trauma, it will always speak louder in your thoughts and actions and eventually affect those surrounding you. Jael looked to school as a way of escape, but little did she know her problems would always follow her until she addressed the root of her issue.

Many of you reading this book may be battling with the side effects of trauma. When I first started writing this book, I thought that it was just for teens. Later I realized that this book is not only for teens but it's also for an adult that never healed the internal girl or boy within that has been affected by adverse childhood experiences (ACEs). Many adults act younger than they are because they never received the help needed after being mistreated or neglected at a young age, which caused some to live their lives in survival mode. Looking at Jael's life before receiving professional help, Jael was living her life in survival mode limited by the grips of fear and anxiety.

Imagine Jael as a young adult with a master's degree in social work preparing for her first professional interview, she's fully confident that the job is already secured but Jael walked into the interview and sees three people staring at her and she immediately goes into survival mode which sends her default mode network into overdrive. When asked by the supervisor, "Tell me a little more about yourself." Jael's brain immediately reverts to her freshmen year in high school, and she bombs the interview and receives a rejected letter the next day. You see unresolved trauma can cause an individual to forfeit opportune blessings. Hidden trauma can make a negative impact on not only one's health but also their success. In the next chapter, we will discuss more side effects of childhood trauma.

Chapter Three

Side Effects

"For God, who commanded the light to shine out of darkness, hath shined in our hearts, to give the light of the knowledge of the glory of God in the face of Jesus Christ."
2 Corinthians 4:6 KJV

Another term often used for trauma is (ACEs) Adverse Childhood Experience. When you visit your doctor, the nurse will ask you questions such as have you ever experienced trauma? Medical Doctors have discovered that Adverse Childhood Experiences have a major impact on the development of an individual life. ACEs are likely events that occur in childhood from the day of conception up until middle adolescence. According to CDC, ACEs are common, about 61% of adults surveyed across just 25 states reported they have experienced at least one type of ACE before age 18, and nearly 1 in 6 reported they had experienced four or more types of ACEs.[4] This does not include the millions of people who are silently living with the effects of trauma.

Trauma can have both a long-term and short-term impact on one's health and success. Someone who has experienced adverse childhood trauma may have difficulty controlling their thoughts, feelings, and emotions. Depending on how severely the individual is

---

[4] Centers for Disease Control and Prevention. *Fast facts: Preventing child sexual*:https://www.cdc.gov/violenceprevention/childsexualabuse/fastfact.html

impacted by trauma as mentioned in the previous chapter, it can cause them to live their life in survivor and/or suicidal mode. I know the first thought that may come to your mind is one constantly thinking about taking their life. I will explain to you briefly what someone's life looks like in suicidal mode.

Survivor mode

Trauma often places an individual into survivor mode so when a challenge comes, they would either fight, flight, or freeze. When you hear fight, flight, or freeze many may think of someone being in serious danger, but in this case, some individuals identify success as a threat. Survivor mode looks like limiting yourself. Instead of being brave and doing something new, you find yourself repeating the same daily routines. Survivor mode can be acquainted with a slave that was given a right to be free but chooses to remain in the same environment because of the fear of the unknown. Their choice can also be due to what we call place attachment, this individual may have developed an emotional bond with a place and now bound themselves to familiarity.

So instead of seizing the moment, they would rather choose bondage over freedom. Many today unintentionally limit themselves. I truly believe that many companies are profiting from the fear of others. You have many individuals that have million-dollar ideas but because they are used to playing it safe in the name of anxiety and fear they miss living the abundant life that was promised to them.

I want to let you know something, this is a very competitive world, like it or not. The world does not care if you have been forced into survivor mode due to childhood trauma. Think about how your life can be impacted if you held back your expertise in a matter that can help your company keep an important grant. How do you think your employer will feel about you if you stay within the limit of safety instead of being an innovator which could help them save the business?

Do you think they will keep the safe employee over the bold employee who gets the job done? They are going to keep the worker that is an asset to their company. I heard a coworker say I'd rather be an asset and not a liability. So always keep that in mind, no matter what stage you are at in life it's important to heal those hidden wounds so that you will not miss out on opportunities to grow.

"No one can limit you but you."

Suicidal mode

Trauma can also cause an individual to live their life in suicidal mode, emotionally they lack the capacity to manage their life. What does this look like? Everything they start they never finish. This person always talks themselves out of an opportunity because of fear. Tries to run from tasks that cause them to step outside of their comfort zone, and when life gets hard, they want to hide and abort every assignment. These individuals would even give up at the peak of success.

"With professional help and belief in yourself, you can overcome the side effects of trauma."

Look at Jael's life, for example, on her first day of school she showed signs of social anxiety. Jael feared public speaking and she struggled with low self-esteem. During her therapy sessions, Jael discovered what was holding her back from being her authentic self. Before therapy Jael was unable to conduct a 5-minute speech without having brain fog or sounding cognitively impaired. She couldn't attend social events with her friends, and she avoided eating breakfast and lunch at school. This is what we call avoidance behavior.

Avoidance behaviors are usually shown in an individual that is challenged with social anxiety; often times they are mistaken to be stuck up. After just three months of therapy Jael's life has changed tremendously, the same classmates that laughed at her are now annoyed that she's always first to get an answer correct when the teacher asks a question.

Anxiety and fear hinder an individual from managing their thoughts, having a coherent speech, completing an easy task and so much more. It's important for parents, leaders, and students to be trauma-informed to know how to respond when they encounter individuals battling a mental disorder. There are four levels of anxiety: mild, moderate, severe, and panic. Take a look at the charts below to learn about the different levels of anxiety and how to identify social anxiety.

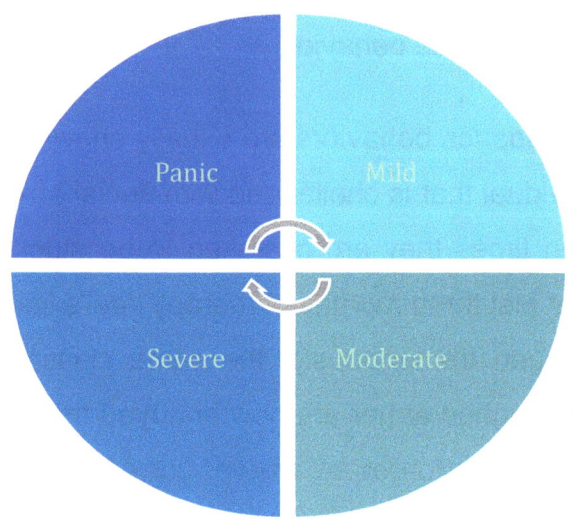

LEVELS OF ANXIETY

Mild and moderate anxiety are more manageable than severe and panic anxiety. They all have the same symptoms but a person with mild to moderate anxiety can immediately combat the symptoms by simply redirecting their thoughts or by using a breathing technique. However, someone with intense anxiety ranging from severe to panic may need medical assistance due to not being able to control physical symptoms. Some of the symptoms of severe to panic anxiety include a rapid, pounding heartbeat, intense sweating, chest pains, and the feeling of their heart being squeezed or pressured.

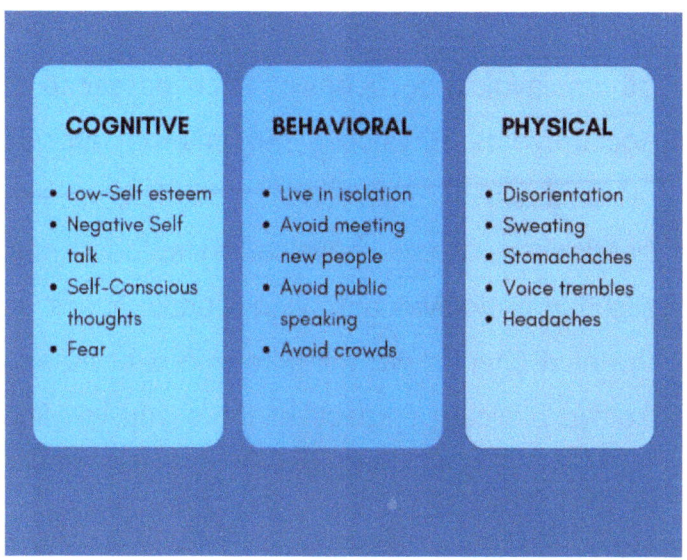

HOW TO IDENTIFY SOCIAL ANXIETY

The chart above gives you a visual of the physical responses to an individual body when challenged with social anxiety. Symptoms of social anxiety fall into three categories. Those categories are cognitive, behavioral, and physical. Social anxiety affects the way a person thinks, behaves, and feels. Mentally the person may have thoughts of feeling inadequate which may result in negative self-talk, doubt, and fear.

Some behaviors an individual challenged with social anxiety may be lack of interactions with others, avoidance behavior such as escaping social events. Physical symptoms may include stomachaches, shaking, diarrhea, and headaches. Some physical symptoms may result in an individual having a panic attack. In the next chapter we will take a look at trauma from a biblical perspective, there you will find that trauma can also be inherited.

Chapter Four

Nothing New Under The Sun

"Trauma is history repeating itself, but you have the authority to break the pattern off your bloodline."

Shaquita Nicole

Generational Trauma

There is nothing new in your life that has not occurred within your bloodline. Think about it for a second and look at your family history. If you begin to dig into your family history, you will discover that many in your family have had similar experiences to you. This is what we call intergenerational trauma. Common symptoms of intergenerational trauma are anxiety, depression, anger, fear, and post-traumatic stress disorder. All symptoms are derived from multiple traumatic events such as domestic violence, substance abuse, sexual abuse, child abuse, poverty, rejection and so much more.

Anything inherited that stunts an individual's growth or causes affliction is often a generational curse. A curse is a negative pattern that can occur more repeatedly in a bloodline. For example, if multiple people in your bloodline are challenged with substance abuse, were sexually assaulted, have been diagnosed with the same mental disorder, or bound with poverty, more than likely that is a curse. I have good news; you or your offspring do not have to be next, it does not matter what ran in your bloodline, know that the curse stops with you.

Curses are released by Satan to oppress God's children. However, because you and I have been redeemed by the blood of the lamb, oppression is no longer our portion. You may be asking yourself what is oppression? Oppression is defined as mental pressure or distress and the state of being subject to unjust treatment or control[5]. **When you are not aware of what is in your bloodline, what's in your bloodline will run you.** God did not create us to live our lives in bondage, he exposes the plans of the so that we can break out. To live the abundant life that God has promised us, we have to address hidden events that has developed into a stronghold within our bloodline. This requires us to open up our mouth and talk about the noticeable toxic traits within our family history.

When you are silent about trauma, the next generation suffers, and the cycle will continue unless someone stands up and breaks it. Many people think that tragic events happen to them because it was divinely orchestrated by God.

---

[5] Oxford Languages and google English Dictionary. (2023)

However, it was never God's plan for His children's souls to be afflicted. We live in an evil world and if we are not spiritually equipped as parents and leaders Satan will take advantage of that. Often times, tragic events are executed within a family through careless decision making. King David life proves that the choices you make can have a negative or positive impact on your bloodline.

In **2 Samuel Chapter 11** you will see that David let his guard down by interfering with Bathsheba and Uriah's marriage. Unknowingly to King David, his affair opened a door and welcomed the spirit of perversion into his home. If you take a look into the family history of David, in **Genesis 34** Jacob and Leah's daughter Dinah was raped. You may be wondering what Jacob has to do with King David. Well to answer your questions King David comes from his bloodline. King David is the descendent of Jacobs fourth son Judah that he had with his wife Leah. So here you see that the spirit of perversion was already in his bloodline waiting for an entry point. Not only did David have an affair but he was also responsible for the death of Uriah.

After the death of Uriah, King David tried to cover up his iniquities, but little did he know that his poor decisions would come back and hunt him. Immediately David's life drastically changed, the first child he had by Bathsheba died and years later, David's daughter was raped by her brother which resulted in a fratricide. In **2 Samuel 13** it is written, after two years of Tamar's assault, Absalom sought revenge on behalf of his sister. Absalom instructed his men to kill his brother Amnon. All of this occurred because David never repented, and his actions displeased God.

Some may say that we are now under a new covenant and once you accept Christ sin and curses are of non-affect, however, that is only contingent upon the believer's stance in Christ and knowledge of the word of God. If you are sinning like David whatever is in your bloodline will hunt you and your children. Before you make a decision it's important to think about how your decisions are going to affect you and your bloodline because that does matter. If decisions didn't matter, we would have never been affected by Adam and Eve's decision when they ate off the tree of the knowledge of good and evil. Your obedience to God is not about you. When you obey God, you set your family up for success. If you are a trauma survivor, what you went through your children will not go through as long as you keep destiny in the forefront of your mind.

"Every decision David made started in the mind first."

Guard Your Mind

When the Bible talks about the heart it is referring to our mind, which controls our thoughts and actions. Instead of being led by the spirit, David was led by his flesh. If David had known that his decisions would cause his very own offspring to be afflicted by Satan, he would have made better choices. Trauma is a tool Satan uses to derail one's destiny. If you haven't noticed, trauma has a major impact on the brain and Satan knows that if he can affect our thought patterns, he can control our lives.

Everything we do starts with our mind. Look at your mind as a door that allows thoughts to enter. Once the thoughts enter your mind, you then begin to act on that thought. It is very important that we control what we allow to enter our minds. **Proverbs 4:23 KJV** *tells us to:* **"Keep thy heart with all diligence; For out of it are the issues of life."** When you guard your mind, you are empowered to make rational decisions. When your mind is clouded with fear, anxiety, and evil thoughts you will make decisions that will affect not only you but generations to come. That's why we have to be proactive so we can avoid having to be reactive.

This leads me to my last point. Exposing Satan brings forth freedom. If people would testify about how they overcame different types of traumas, what they experienced will save other lives. Testimonies are a powerful tool against Satan because they abort his plans to destroy someone's destiny and bring forth deliverance to an individual that was bound by the same experience. In order to break any curse, you have to first identify it then call it out. Staying silent does not eliminate trauma. ***The longer you live your life in repression the longer you give trauma permission to dominate.***

Satan uses your silence as a leverage to keep you muzzled, which looks like remaining silent when you are supposed to speak up and it causes you to think that your opinion does not matter to your family, peers, coworkers, or community. A similar term for muzzled is suppress, when someone is suppressed, they are limited, limited in their thinking, finances, relationships, and careers. That does not have to be your story, so speak up.

If trauma has led you away from God, I want you to know that it was never God's plan for you to experience that pain. God said in **Jeremiah 29:11 AMP states: that the plans and thoughts He has for you are good, and He has plans of peace and well-being that is not for disaster and that will give you a future and hope. In Jeremiah 31:3 AMP He goes on to say**: "I have loved you with an everlasting love; Therefore, with lovingkindness I have drawn you *and* continued my faithfulness to you." **God wants you, to come back to Him and He will restore your soul for His name's sake according to Psalm 23, your deliverance brings honor to God's name.** If you find yourself right now in a dark space feeling as if you are alone or that you are not worthy of God's love or His provision, I want you to say this prayer below and rededicate or give your life to Christ.

SAY THIS PRAYER OF RESTORATION: *Father, I repent for allowing pain to pull me away from you. In the name of Jesus, I ask you today to deliver me from all iniquities. I invite you back into my life. I confess with my mouth and believe in my heart that Jesus died for my sins. Take the throne of my heart, take the throne of my mind, revive me Father, fill me with Holy Spirit and make me new again. Amen.*

Generational Blessings

I cannot end this chapter without talking about generational blessings. Not everyone's bloodline is plagued with curses, you have some families that were fortunate enough to have forefathers that didn't engage in demonic activities. They read the word and applied the word to their lives.

If you grew up on a rocky foundation, it's ok, you now have a mandate on your life to reverse the curse and replace it with generational blessings by applying what you learn to your life and by obeying God's word. **Proverbs 11:9 KJV states: "But through knowledge shall the just be delivered."** So, let's take a look at God's track record of blessing those that trust and obeyed Him. Many of you have heard of Hannah's story. In first Samuel Hannah was believing God for a child, she was fed up with being mocked, so she cried out to the Lord and asked him for a son, and in **1 Samuel 1:11** she made a vow that she would give him back to God.

The Lord received Hannah's vow and answered her prayers. After Hannah gave Samuel back to the Lord years later in **1 Samuel 2:21 KJV states that "And the Lord visited Hannah, so that she conceived, and bare three sons and two daughters. And the child Samuel grew before the Lord."** The Hebrew word for grew is (gadal), which means to grow, become great or important, promote, make powerful, and do great things. So, because of Hannah's vow Samuel was favored by God. I believe that Hannah's sacrifice provoked the gift of obedience upon Samuel. Samuel was known as a man of integrity according to **1 Samuel 3:19 KJV states "And Samuel grew, and the LORD was with him, and did let none of his words fall to the ground."**

Another person we can look at is Abraham, because of Abraham obedience when asked by the Lord to sacrifice his only son. Not only was Isaac saved but according to **Galatians 3:9** because of Abraham obedience we are also partakers of the reward Abraham was given after obeying God. Finally, because of the sacrifice Jesus made we can live a life of freedom and abundance. God is a covenant keeping God, so just as he kept Hannah, Samuel and Abraham He is keeping us too. Our obedience to God unlocks the doors of Heaven, **Hebrew 8:6** tells us that we are now under a better covenant and the covenant is established on better promises. Those promises includes the glory-to-glory experience that God promised us in **2 Corinthians 3:18 AMP.** However, disobedience will hinder you from receiving the blessings of God. It's better to Obey God than to make unnecessary sacrifices.

Chapter Five

Be Proactive

"The moment you wait for someone else to speak up is the moment you give trauma permission to repeat."
Shaquita Nicole

Awareness

I truly believe that adverse childhood experiences are the number one cause of broken and unhealthy individuals, especially when trauma is left unaddressed. To prevent the cycle of abuse in our homes and communities we must raise awareness in our communities by addressing the issue and stop ignoring the signs of trauma. Some of the possible warning signs of trauma in adolescents are changes in emotional and physical reactions such as

- Self-destructive behavior (drinking too much, attempting suicide, or self-injury such as cutting)
- Trouble sleeping.
- Trouble concentrating.
- Irritability, angry outbursts, or aggressive behavior.
- Overwhelming guilt or shame.

Of course, not all traumatic events are controllable, for instance natural disasters or world events. My main focus in this chapter is to address sexual abuse and ways to prevent this event from occurring in your home or community. Sexual abuse is known for being ignored, due to shame many push sexual abuse under the rug and will often take the pain to their graves instead of speaking up.

Sexual abuse is one of the most underreported crimes in the US. Survivors of sexual abuse are less likely to report their perpetrator due to fear and shame. According to research "A common myth is that child sexual abuse is perpetrated by strangers and pedophiles. But most people who sexually abuse children are prone to be friends, partners, family members, and community members. Research studies also show around 93 percent of children who are victims of sexual abuse are familiar with their abuser. Less than 10 percent of sexually abused children are abused by a stranger.[6] Now that is something to think about.

We have to be mindful of the environments we allow our children to be in. Senseless mistakes become an easy avenue for Satan to damage

---

[6] *Perpetrators of sexual violence:*

*Statistics.*www.rainn.org/statistics/perpetrators-sexual-violence

an innocent child. This can place a child at risk of growing up broken or confused about their identity, like Jael. Parents, if you allow your child to visit others or attend sleepovers, you want to make sure that there will be proper supervision and that your child is old enough to communicate.

Disclaimer, I am not encouraging anyone to operate in fear, my main goal is to bring awareness of an issue that many shy away from addressing. As believers, we have to be sensitive and awakened to the devices of Satan. His mission is to kill our children's dreams, steal their identities, and destroy their destinies. You learned in the previous chapter that Satan uses trauma as a gateway to destroy one's future. So be very attentive to the well-being of your child.

Interventions

Prayer is another way to stop trauma from repeating, when I say pray, I don't mean to worry. When you pray you are simply having a conversation with God like you would have with your children. However, make sure when you pray that you are not praying in fear, pray from a place of knowing that your Father hears you and He will respond. Even after you pray Satan will try to lie to you and say it didn't work but all you have to do is rebuke him because he doesn't have the final say, God does. Do not underestimate the power of prayer, your prayers alone can stop hell's assignment from being fulfilled in your life and your children's life. God never changes, so if He did it for Hannah and Jael, He will do the same for you.

In order to see the hand of God move in your family's life you have to have a relationship with Him through his word. Just as God has a plan for our destiny Satan has a plan too, but it cannot prevail when we have a relationship with God and are led by Holy Spirit. As a child of God, we are always supposed to be ahead and not behind, God will always warn you before destruction occurs but it's only through relationship with Him, we are able to receive the benefits.

If you were sexually assaulted at a young age and you desire children or have children, a prayer is attached below for you. Prayer is a powerful prevention tool, once you pray rest in God knowing that he answered your prayers. Know without a doubt in your mind that the generational cycle of sexual trauma has been broken off your bloodline.

Warfare Prayer: *In the name of Jesus, I cancel every wicked agenda Hell has assigned to my bloodline. I decree and declare a wall of fire around my children. In Zechariah 2:5 KJV you said in your word that you will be unto my child/children a wall of fire around them, and you will be the glory in the midst of them. In Jesus name, I decree, and I declare the Lord's will shall prevail over hell for my children's destiny. In Job 22:28 KJV you said we shall decree a thing, and it shall be established unto us: and your* *light shall shine upon thy ways. By the power and authority of Jesus Christ I send arrows of fire to the spirit of perversion, and any generational sex demon that is assigned to my children's destiny. I declare today every evil appointment is canceled. Oh Lord, I ask that you release your warring Angels to go before my child/children and war on their behalf. In Psalm 91:11 you said that you give your Angels charge over my child/children to keep them in all their ways. I thank you Lord for going before my child/children and making every crooked path straight just as you said in Isaiah 45:2 KJV. In Jesus mighty name I pray, amen.*

Educate

When it comes to sexual assault prevention, it's extremely important that you also educate your children as well. Explain to them what good and bad touches are. Teach them what safety boundaries are and let them know that it is ok to tell anybody NO when someone tries to break their safety boundaries. For example, it is okay to tell someone:

- No, you cannot touch my private area.
- No, you cannot show me your private part.
- No, I do not want to sit on your lap.
- No, I do not keep secrets.
- No, I do not want to watch inappropriate videos.
- No, I do not want to touch your private area.

I believe you can start talking to your children about this as early as the age of five. Some people may say the age of five is too young to learn such a thing, but they are not. If you don't teach them then their classmates that have been exposed to inappropriate acts at their age will.

We cannot be naive, today we have babies born in a world of fast-paced technology. So, educate your children, but of course, use wisdom when doing so and communicate with them to their level. Don't just ask your children weird questions out of fear. When you educate your children, you are letting them know that you care about them. You want to create a safe space for your children to have an open dialogue with you at an early age.

This prevents them from being misled by others. Leaders, you too are obligated to teach our youth what is right and wrong, **one moment, one word, one person can change someone's destiny** and that person can be you! If possible, it is detrimental that we protect our children, as well as other children from emotional and physical harm. If you see something wrong, say something, don't have a "minding my own business mentality."

Mentorship

Mentorship is another way to be proactive in our youth lives. Mentorship gives our youth an advantage in life. It allows them to avoid certain mistakes that can cause set back and delays. As leaders and parents, we must always push our youth into being the best version of themselves.

There are many adolescents like Jael who are suffering in silence waiting to graduate so that they can escape their toxic environment. Unfortunately, some do not make it out, due to thinking the only way out is to take their life or ruin it by making careless decisions that will alter their destiny for the worse. There are also some adults like Mrs. Deborah, who was resilient enough to fight through the pain and still became successful, and there are some that allow pain to paralyze them, which becomes a hindrance to their success. As professionals, and leaders, we have a chance to make a difference in a young person's life.

Parents, if your child may have been abused physically, or sexually, the best way to assist them is by providing him/her with the appropriate resources as early as possible to prevent long-term damages. So do not normalize abnormal behavior, if you notice that your child/children may need help in any area of their life that will improve their academic and social skills, start seeking help as soon as possible to make sure they thrive in those areas.

Mentors can support our youth in community based or school-based settings by assisting them with making healthy choices and discovering who they are to achieve their potential. To accomplish this as mentors, parents and leaders we must be selfless and equipped to identify when our teens are hurting verses being an introvert or rebellious. 1:1 support group session is also a great source to build an adolescent social skills and confidence while also learning to build trust.

At risk youth tend to have trust issues after experiencing trauma at such a young age, so many would immediately build a wall of self-protection as a defense mechanism. This hinders an adolescent from learning how to build healthy relationship and eventually once they enter into adulthood walls of self-protection can hinder one from accepting God ordained opportunities just so that they can stay within their comfort zone. I believe exposure is also a key to breaking barriers off of their life. Due to lack of exposure, just like a toddler they will only imitate what they see and never soar beyond the norm within their environment.

If you see any warning signs that were listed above within an adolescent that affects their day-to-day functioning, it's important to start early intervention by way of recommending psychotherapy or seeking some form of professional assistance. Any trauma that is not addressed has a negative impact on a person's behavior and future. In the next chapter, you will learn about the importance of seeking help.

Chapter Six
Seek Help

"Have I not commanded you? Be strong and of good courage; do not be afraid, nor be dismayed, for the Lord your God is with you wherever you go."
Joshua 1:9 NKJV

Stigma

Due to a lack of awareness and education, there are many stigmas around mental health, which causes an individual to avoid seeking professional help. Stigma against mental health comes from family, friends, and coworkers. You may hear people challenged with depression labeled as lazy, or you may hear someone being called slow if they are challenged with a mental disorder that causes cognitive impairment. These are all stereotypes that often result in an individual internalizing the negative responses of those around them, this is called self-stigma. Instead of seeking help, the individual starts to have negative ideas or attitudes about themselves.

Don't allow fear, shame, or pride to keep you from seeking help. To my brothers and sisters in Christ prayer alone does not resolve trauma. Even when Elijah was in a state of depression the Lord consoled him. When you experience trauma at a young age it affects your soul, which is your mind, will, and emotions. In some way, what happened to you shaped the way you think and how you respond to people and problems.

You may not notice it because you have made a negative behavior pattern your norm. For example, some people that have experienced complex trauma may have trust issues, a hard time connecting with people they don't know, or only feel comfortable around people they are familiar with. This is a self-defense mechanism and God didn't create us to walk around with fences up. Another one is shutting down on people when they hurt or say something that offended you, this can be your nuclear family, wife, husband, your friends, and coworkers. This response is an unhealthy defense mechanism, you must learn how to communicate with those that unknowingly hurt you or intentionally hurt you.

It is not healthy to be so easily offended. **Offense is a spirit that can stunt your growth.** It will cause you to take everything personal and prevents you from not being able to develop pure relationships, this can be with the people your voice is assigned to and also with those who are called to you. Which will result in never receiving all that God has for you because often times the spirit of offense cause resentment and the root of resentment is unforgiveness. **Hebrews 12:14-15 KJV** instructs us to: *"Follow peace with all men, and holiness, without which no man shall* *see the Lord: Looking diligently lest any man fail of the grace of God; lest any root of bitterness springing up trouble you, and thereby many be defiled."*

If Jael had blocked Mrs. Deborah out of her life, she would have denied herself access to freedom from everything that was oppressing her, not only that but her environment would have never shifted. How many times have you pushed someone away? That means you well but because of offense you ignored their advice, so you learned the hard way when you didn't have to. That's what offense does, it controls your destiny and prevents you from breaking barriers. That's why it is so important to be led by the spirit and not by our flesh. The flesh craves bondage and the spirit thirsts for freedom, choose which one you will serve. One of the definitions of serve is to give a helping hand to someone, are you going to help your flesh or help your spirit?

Use Wisdom

Before seeking help, you want to first pray and ask the Lord to lead you to the right therapist for you and do your research. You don't want to waste your time and money hearing from someone that is not equipped for your situation. Its's important to include God in on your healing journey because apart from Him there is no true healing. When we choose God's way of healing, we are not just learning how to cope with the issue, but we learn how to break free and walk in total healing and deliverance. If you live in an area where resources are limited there are also virtual therapy services available that are just as impactful as in-person meetings.

See Something Say Something

When it comes to sexual abuse incidents, report the crime immediately. Don't be embarrassed or concerned about what people will say in the community. Remember your silence will cause the next generation to suffer. If you are a professional who is mandated to report sexual abuse, make sure to write a report to your local child protective service office immediately. On page 63 and 64, you learned that sexual abuse is the most underreported case in the U.S., one reason being is because of the lack of credible evidence.

After a sexual assault incident occurs, victims are asked to preserve all physical evidence, contact an officer, withhold from taking a bath, and seek medical care immediately at a local hospital that conducts a rape kit, known as a Sexual Assault Evidence Kit. The content of the kit varies by state and jurisdiction. If you live in an area where SAEKs are not available, make sure you allow the officers to collect all DNA samples. Without credible evidence crimes like this are often unsubstantiated. [7]

---

[7] What is a sexual assault forensic exam? RAINN: https://www.rainn.org/articles/rape-kit

Deliverance

Getting therapeutic assistance is a good first step in the direction towards healing, but as a believer of Jesus Christ I also recommend inner healing and deliverance. How do you know if you need inner healing and deliverance? One main indication is if you have been a believer for years or may have sought therapy but yet you are still bound to the symptoms of trauma, that is an indication that you need inner healing and deliverance. If you have no knowledge in this area, I advise you to seek wise counsel. Deliverance is another topic that many avoid because of the stigma.

Deliverance is needed for everyone that is battling with any form of oppression, especially if they experienced child maltreatment. Child maltreatment includes all types of abuse from conception up until 18. Each abuse is a gateway for Satan to alter an individual identity and their behavior. Many do not believe that it is possible for a believer of Christ Jesus to be demonically oppressed, however it is. If it was not possible Christians wouldn't be dying from suicide.

Hidden wounds give Satan legal access to control one's destiny. As mentioned in previous chapters, trauma has a major impact on an individual life, physically, mentally, emotionally, and spiritually. It's imperative that these hidden wounds are addressed so that you can live the life of freedom that God promised us here on earth. After you are healed, you are equipped to assist others that are bound. Which leads me to my last point, your healing is not just about you, it's about those who are coming behind you and generations to come.

You are more effective in the lives of others when you are healed. There is a saying that hurt people hurt people. This is so true whether it may be intentional or not. So, take a bold step today and address the hidden wounds in your life. At the end of this book, the author also listed more resources that are available nationwide. As recommended consult with God first so that you can see a transformation in your life. For the individual reading this book that may not have a relationship with God, I want to let you know that you too have a chance to receive total freedom, by first surrendering your life to Christ. Once you surrender your life to Christ you become empowered to break free from the cycles of mental distress.

CHAPTER 7

POWER OF WORDS

"The tongue can bring death or life; those who love to talk will reap the consequences."

PROVERBS 18:21 NLT

Many of us have quoted the scripture that life and death lie in the power of the tongue but are rarely cautious of what we say to others and even ourselves. Due to psychological reasons, negative moments in life can affect an individual's future. As mentioned, this is one reason we see so many adults that have the personality of a child because one negative moment had a long-lasting detrimental effect on their life. The effects of negative words include poor self-esteem, self-defeating behavior, anxiety, limited mindset, insecurity, perfectionism, and failure.

It's important to think before you speak because your response can destroy someone's destiny. Throughout the beginning of this book, you see that Jael life was impacted by words both negative and positive. In her home she was devalued by her family and at her previous school she was misunderstood, every negative word that was spoken over her life shaped the way she viewed herself. It wasn't until Jael met Mrs. Deborah that her life began to change. All Mrs. Deborah did was speak life into her. Mrs. Deborah was not just babbling off, but her words planted seeds into Jael that eventually produced good fruit. Just as Mrs. Deborah poured into Jael, as leaders and parents we are subject to do the same.

On the first day of meeting Jael, Mrs. Deborah could have easily gotten offended and spoke negatively about her, but Mrs. Deborah knew the importance of words. She could have put Jael out of class but instead she allowed her to feel how she felt in the moment and corrected her in love later. After that day Jael never disrespected Mrs. Deborah again. When we pour into our teens from a pure place our action alone enforces our youth to correct their negative behavior. It may take more time for some, but the majority will be captivated by the love and kindness that you are showing them.

I can imagine someone thinking, **what if I never had anyone to encourage me like Mrs. Deborah and grew up being beat down by peers, family, and educators, rather uplifted?** If you never had anyone to encourage you before, I want you to do something not for me or anyone else but for yourself. Learn how to encourage yourself in the Lord, just as David did in the midst of being threatened to be stoned by men he trusted.

Just to give a quick background of this story David and his men were just returning home after winning a battle, but when everybody made it home, they all realized that their home was vandalized, and their family were abducted. So, the men got upset with David and plotted to take him out. Instead of trying to defend himself, in **1 Samuel 30:6-8KJV,** the word states that David was greatly distressed, but despite the threats David encouraged himself in the Lord. He understood that if he inquired of the Lord, he would come through for not only him but for the men that were trying to stone him too. And guess what, God gave David the strength he needed to pursue, overtake his enemies, and recover all that was taking away from him and his soldiers.

Just as David encouraged himself and received strength and a strategy to defeat his enemies so can you with the power of your words. **Matthew 12:34 AMP states "the mouth speaks out of which fills the heart."** So, the question is what do you think about yourself and what are you saying to yourself? In the following pages, I provided a list of affirmations and prayers to strengthen you as a leader, parent, or teen. Prayer and affirmations promote positive self-changes and changes the way you think about yourself. As we have learned in this chapter that our words have power which can change our lives for the better or for the worse. So don't just read the affirmations and prayers but activate the words by using them as a daily tool you need every day. Reference back to these tools as many times as you need to. Because we are going to end this cycle of **HIDDEN TRAUMA IN PLAIN SIGHT.**

Affirmations for Teens

I am not what happened to me.

I am valuable.

I know who I am.

I am whom God says I am.

I was fearfully and wonderfully made.

I was created for a purpose and that purpose will be fulfilled.

Greatness rests upon my life.

My identity is secured in Christ.

There is nothing too hard for me.

I start and finish everything strong.

Quitting is not in my DNA.

I am more than a conqueror.

Affirmations for Leaders

I am whole in Christ.

I have a sound mind.

I am not afraid of the unknown.

I am unstoppable.

I am relentless for Christ.

I am empowered by Holy Spirit to lead effectively.

I am spirit led and not emotionally driven.

I am alert and awaken to the needs of others.

I am a Kingdom philanthropist.

I lead with integrity.

I do not compromise to make others feel comfortable.

I am not obsessed with the applause of man.

My identity is secured in Christ.

Affirmations for Parents

I am anointed to lead my family.

I am empowered to shift the atmosphere of my home.

I am a wise parent that is attentive to not only my needs but my family needs.

I am selfless.

I am the head and not the tail.

My family and I are abundantly supplied.

Wealth and riches reside in our home.

I can do all things with Christ.

My family and I lack no good thing.

I am healthy, whole, and delivered.

I am loved by my family.

I am a blessing to my family and not a burden.

I am confident the Lord will complete what he started in me.

Prayers for Teens

Father in the name of Jesus I thank you for creating me in your image and likeness. I accept the way you made me, and I renounce the false identity Satan gave me. I decree and declare I have a mind of Christ concerning my life. I am a leader. I am not an attention seeker. In Jesus' name, I disassociate myself with people-pleasing, pride, and fear. In Jesus's name, I come out of agreement with every ungodly title. I decree and declare I am free, confident, I am unbreakable, I am bold, and I am courageous. I decree and declare I am walking in authority because the great I am lives inside of me. God, I am confident that you have begun a good work in me, and you are faithful to perform. Amen!

Prayer for Teachers

Father in the name of Jesus I thank you for entrusting me to lead the next generation. Father, I ask that you help me to be a good steward over those you have placed into my care. In the name of Jesus, I decree and declare every student that enters my classroom life will be changed. I decree and declare no one is a failure in my classroom. My students are more than conquerors. Classroom _____ is the top class at _____. Classroom _____ produces successful students. Every student in classroom _____ was uniquely and wonderfully made by God. Father, I thank you for teaching me how to be an effective leader for our future leaders. Amen

Prayer for Leaders

Father in the name of Jesus I thank you for creating me to be a leader. Father, I ask that you give me grace and wisdom to lead effectively in my home, on my job, and in my community. Father God, I ask you to clothe me in humility and remove any pride within my heart. Give me your heart for those you have entrusted me to lead. May every individual that connects with me encounter your love, your joy, and peace. Amen!

Prayer for Parents

Father in the name of Jesus, I thank you for my child/children. Father God, I ask that you give me the grace and wisdom I need to be a godly example in my children/ child's life. When my child/children depart from me I trust that you will protect them from evil. According to Psalm 91 Lord, you said no evil shall befall them nor shall any plague come near their dwelling, you said that you will cover my child/ children with your feathers, and under your wings, they will find refuge; my child/ children will not fear the terror of night, nor the arrow that flies by day. Father in the name of Jesus I decree and declare you are my child/children pillar of cloud by day and their fire by night. You said in Psalm 35:1 that you will contend against those who contend against my child/ children. Father, I am not blind to 's agenda, I ask that you set a watch over my child/children's ears and eyes. I decree and declare my child/children's eyes and ears will not become tainted with demonic activities. I ask that you surround my child/ children with godly men and women after your heart, if any evil is present within their vicinity, I ask that you release my child/children warring angels to protect them from the darkness of this world. In Jesus' name, I pray, Amen.

Helpful Resources and Nationwide Resources

Better help (Virtual Therapy)

Dial 211 for your local resources and essential services

Disaster Distress Helpline: 1-800-985-5990

Domestic Violence Hotline: 1-800-799-7233

SAMHSA's National Helpline: 1-800-662-HELP (4357)

Substance Abuse and Mental Health Services: 1-800-273-TALK

National Sexual Assault Hotline: 1-800-656-HOPE (4673)

National Suicide Prevention Lifeline: Dial 988 to reach a trained Crisis Counselor

References

Oppression Definition: Oxford Languages and google English Dictionary. www.oed.com (2023)

Centers for Disease Control and Prevention. (2022, April 6). Fast facts: Preventing child sexual abuse/ violence prevention injury Center CDC. Centers for Disease Control and Prevention. Retrieved May 6, 2023, from https://www.cdc.gov/violenceprevention/childsexualabuse/fastfact.html

Child sexual abuse. RAINN. (n.d.). Retrieved May 6, 2023, from https://www.rainn.org/articles/child-sexual-abuse

Perpetrators of sexual violence: Statistics. RAINN. (n.d.). Retrieved May 6, 2023, from https://www.rainn.org/statistics/perpetrators-sexual-violence

What are the 3 types of trauma? Mental Health Center of San Diego. (2022, November 30). Retrieved from https://mhcsandiego.com/types-of-trauma/

www.ingramcontent.com/pod-product-compliance
Lightning Source LLC
Chambersburg PA
CBHW071157090426
42736CB00012B/2359